A LIFE WELL LIVED

A GIFT OF PRESENCE

A COLLECTION OF QUOTES BY

HAROLD S. GOODMAN

A LIFE WELL LIVED
A Gift of Presence

A collection of quotes by

Harold S. Goodman

MARINER
PUBLISHING

BUENA VISTA, VIRGINIA

1 3 5 7 9 10 8 6 4 2

Library of Congress Control Number: 2007943848

A Life Well Lived
Harold S. Goodman
p. cm.
1. Philosophy 2. Quotations

I. Goodman, Harold S. 1926— II. Title.
ISBN 13: 978-0-9800077-3-2 (softcover : alk. paper)
ISBN 10: 0-9800077-0-7

Mariner Publishing
A division of
Mariner Companies, Inc.
131 West 21st ST.
Buena Vista, VA 24416
Tel: 540-264-0021
http://www.marinermedia.com

Dedicated to:

Elsie Mae, who is the most wonderful woman — and she's my wife.

Life was meant to be a celebration of a miracle.

Definition of Life: a dimensionless sphere of unending possibilities.

Love is the greatest praise and affirmation human beings can bestow on one another.

One must enjoy the love of others to appreciate the love of God.

Honesty is good, but sincerity is so much better because it comes out of your mouth so much smoother.

Sincerity is one of the most appealing expressions a person can demonstrate to another.

One may well experience a glint of appreciation on a moment's notice, but full appreciation of the moment, must require a lifetime of wakefulness.

A comment to all us fanatics who wish to change the world.

. . Our time would best be spent on preparing our own body, mind, heart, and soul, for this journey through life rather than seeing to others.

I want the job of chief advocate for some or all of the people with the aim of creating a better world, by preserving what there is and having people respecting themselves and others.

MANKIND'S CONTINUAL DESIRE TO MAKE LIFE EASIER IS BECOMING THE BASIS FOR MANKIND'S ULTIMATE DESTRUCTION.

When you have to make a choice, choose the one that is most personal.

PHYSICAL FITNESS MUST OCCUR FROM THE INSIDE OUT... BEGINNING WITH A STRONG DESIRE FROM WITHIN.

STRETCHING IS THE BEGINNING OF STRENGTHENING.

No one ever listens until it's way too late.

PHYSICAL FITNESS AT ANY AGE IS
WHEN YOU CAN MOVE ANY WAY
YOU WANT WITHOUT FEAR OF PAIN.

Everyone must be a Peacock in their own way.

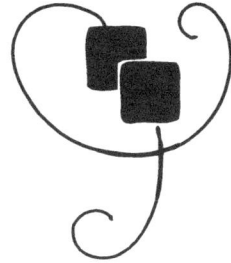

The foundation of sickness is being jumbled about what is most important in life.

GROW OLD WITH *a passion!*

I REALIZE I AM OLD ENOUGH NOW TO KNOW THAT I DON'T HAVE TO LOOK PRETTY ANYMORE TO LOOK GOOD.

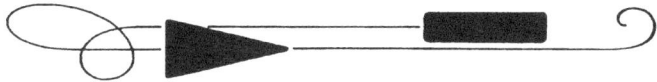

When I was younger, I would be satisfied if I was happy once in a while, but now that I'm actually getting old, I want to be happy all the time.

If today is not a learning experience, just how much can you expect to learn in the future.

There is no question in my mind I am a very, very slow learner, but I must admit it served me well.

You can ask anything you want of another person as long as you are willing to accept yes or no for an answer.

WHATEVER YOU NEGLECT TODAY, YOU WILL CONFRONT TOMORROW.

CORRUPTION IS THE ABILITY TO TAINT OR CONTAMINATE A SUBSTANCE OF GREAT PURITY; AND BENEFIT.

I think that the voice inside my head is getting smarter; if I'm not mistaken.

It is one thing to get peoples attention; what you do with it is a whole other matter.

From my thoughts I have woven my life; from our thoughts we fashion our world.

If you want to know the truth, nearly everyone is living right next to wonderful.

My family is my heart throb.

Because of you, I want to take my next breath.

ENLIGHTMENT IS THE ABILITY TO POUR YOUR HEART INTO EVERY MOMENT.

I WANT TO SEE THE EXPRESSIONS OF PEOPLES' HEARTS.

What I am is a legend in my own mind.

A warrior will speak the truth without flinching; a skilled warrior will speak the truth without offending.

Everyone should have faith in the value of their individual uniqueness.

The essence of love is propinquity. (pro-pin-qui-ty: nearness in time or place, nearness of relationship; kinship)

ELSIE MAE IS THE MOST WONDERFUL WOMAN — AND SHE'S MY WIFE.

FOR OUR CHILDREN, CARING AND REGARD ULTIMATELY TURN TO LOVE AND RESPECT.

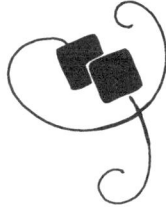

Love is in the air and an act of love exudes a quality which flavors any action —whatvever it might be.

In a perfect life, the nearer the end, the sweeter and more meaningful the experience.

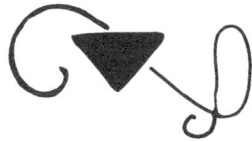

Hard to even imagine we live in a place surrounded by a space so vast it can only be thought of as endless and everywhere.

IN THE ANNALS OF "GOOD DAYS," THIS DAY IS A PERFECT DAY OF COUNTRY LIVING.

Perfect is when you can't imagine anything better.

When our son looks back on his childhood, I wish for him to be able to say, "they showed me what it means to be happy."

When I said, "God, my life is in your hands," he answered, "No, it's in yours."

If you are going to lie on this world to anybody... you can rest assured that the first one lied to, is going to be you.

With age, it is perfectly appropriate to focus your attention to the more personal aspects of life... like your inside and outside.

One must consciously demand more from our body... certainly not less.

THE OLDER YOU GET, THE MORE YOU ARE RESPONSIBLE FOR WHO AND WHAT YOU ARE.

Beauty is beauty "anyway you see it."

Once the bonds of inertia are broken, even mountains can be moved.

When we as a society finally subscribe to a common cause or action, we invariably carry each of them to some ridiculous extreme.

Human science is showing us there is no limit too little, and no limit too big.

Having a sweetheart is why old men want to live to be older.

In true love, intimacy is like being invited into a magnificent home where all the doors are open.

Doing things just doesn't get it; loving what you're doing is much more to the point.

We each are born to discover life in an ever changing world.

As we grow older our minds become filled with endless instructions... to the point there is hardly any room left for examining what is actually going on.

Amazing the bafflement our minds offer when considering "what life is all about."

A prophet is someone who feels they see the truths of life and feels compelled to share their thoughts to whomever is willing to listen.

The best of the best feelings:
I'm given all the love I've ever
wanted.

Just remember, the world is not going to stand still, waiting for you to catch up.

The most intimate things in life are the most important.

An I.O.U. to your sweetheart: No matter how much you love me... I will always love you more.

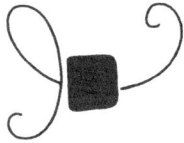

ELSIE MAE AND I ARE NOT FAMOUS, BUT WE ARE DEDICATED HUMAN BEINGS.

The kind of child we leave behind is our personal message to the future.

What am I doing with my life?
I'm learning how to live with
the woman I love the most.

To find your true love you must become the kind of person you so wistfully desire.

Love gives you the best appetite for life.

Lovers must spend more and more time together if they want to learn and experience all the intricate attributes of true love.

WITH MY MEMORIES BEING SHREDDED, I AM MORE AND MORE A CAPTIVE TO THE PRESENT.

Few people appreciate the profundity of everyday life.

ALMOST every thing we do can be improved with time and experience.

I've never tried to be more than just an everyday good man.

Being an expert of one kind or another does not guarantee a happy life.

I've always strived to look young and handsome... now that I am over 80 years old, I can only hope for wise and gracious.

The goal is to live life to the best of our understanding rather than following the dictates of other people from other times.

A prayer is a desire taken to the point of wanting it with all of one's mind, body, and soul... like my wife said about wanting our baby.

The way you slow your life down so you can enjoy it is to focus your attention to the details.

THE DETAILED STATE OF OUR MINDS SUBTLY FLAVORS OUR LIVES, MOMENT BY MOMENT.

Now that we can practically communicate with everyone wouldn't it be nice if someone had something worthwhile to say?

It appears that the ultimate goal of our current economic system is to reduce our environment to it's chemical components and sell them, one at a time, to the highest bidders.

The only significant way mankind has changed in thousands of years, is the content of our thoughts.

Poise is an attitude of pleasant waiting.

THE COMMON ELEMENT OF ANY CHALLENGE IS A THOUGHT-PROVOKING SITUATION.

I can not imagine a conflict between "mans" conscience and "God's" will.

Having a vision of a wonderful life is the first step in its creation.

The greater freedom one enjoys, the greater responsibility one must exercise.

Social conscience: the single most important thing a person can do is to be a role model for those people around you.

Time and attention given by a loved one, makes life worthwhile - moment by moment.

Belief in miracles: If I can find something wonderful in everyday life, how can I not believe in miracles.

If your expectations are too low, then you're pretty much stuck with what you've got.

ENLIGHTMENT: Everyone has had an inspired moment... enlightment is merely a bunch of these moments strung together into an event and eventually into a life.

In every twist and turn, life is forever giving; but forever demanding.

The depth and meaningfulness of love is directly related to understanding and appreciation.

What everyone wants is recognition and acknowledgement.

On optimism:

I'm planning on the last day of my life, being the best day of my life.